For the Love of God

Victoria E Southard

ISBN:
ISBN-13: 978-1513627830

DEDICATION

I would like to dedicate this book to my family who supports my beliefs and have backed me from day one on this creative journey.

And to Mrs. Miller my 5th grade teacher for loving me when other didn't or wouldn't.

CONTENTS

Chapter 1

Boulders in our Way

March 16, 1973, I will never remember this day as opposed to me never forgetting that day. On this day while many others were preparing for the upcoming celebration of St. Patrick's Day, my beautiful parents were welcoming me into this world. My older brother, not so much since I was a girl.

I didn't come peacefully I came into this world kicking and fighting the whole way. Guess I wasn't ready to leave Heaven yet. However, everyone else forced me to enter into this unknown world, and I can say I don't think I was in love with the idea.

My birth wasn't particularly easy for my mama. I ripped and tore her as I tried to keep from being forced into this world. Well more like I had a big head, but it sounds more dramatic the other way.

I may be in my forties now, but I can still remember the carefreeness of life as a small child. My fears were monstrous and my happiness full. I remember that it didn't matter where I lived or what my house was like, as long as I had my toys and felt safe I was AOK.

We moved from Wisconsin to Hawaii and back to Wisconsin all by the time I was two. I have only vague memories of Hawaii, like sifting for pooka shells on the beach with my mama and watching her make family and friends back home a pooka necklaces. I remember the plastic containers that mom saved from cooking and she would fill them with pooka shells.

While we were living in Hawaii, we lived on the beach on the island of Oahu, off the King Kamehameha Highway. However, I didn't like water, and to this day I still can't stand it in large amounts or if it has living things in it. It scares the bajeebers out of me.

I have a saying I once heard that if you get attacked by a shark in the water, well that's not a shark attack. If you are in your hotel room and a shark comes up to your room and attacks you then THAT is a shark attack. Best just for me to stay away from areas where I am not the top of the food chain. That is a good rule of thumb for anyone. I know I shouldn't fear things and should rely on God's power and love to always keep me safe. However, it seems to me that if I jump into a river of crocs, then God would probably be like, "Well daughter I gave you a boat, I gave you land, I protected you, and you still managed to get eaten by crocs." Yup, that's my luck.

However, on the other hand, my phobia of water (and mostly the things in the water) keep me safe on shore.

In Hawaii, my parents said that when I was playing on the beach in the sand that I wouldn't even have to look up to know what size the wave was. I would just be playing and then take a few steps back and never look up and never get my feet wet. I seemed to always be one step ahead of the waves coming in.

I also love to have my pet's around me daily. See in Hawaii, when the moon comes out the geckos would cover the windows. And in the morning the geckos that loved me the most stayed and waited for me to get up and get them. They would let me carry them around all day, and I would put them in little boxes or build houses for them out of the sand. Those little guys sure did love me. They never bit or peed or pooped on me. In fact, they didn't do much of anything at all but sleep. Guess they were just tired from the night's excitement. Every day a new one would be waiting for me, and the cycle would start all over again.

We moved back to Wisconsin when I was two or three. My dad was always handy at fixing cars. One night he was working on his car in the parking lot where we lived. He left the car running while he went inside to get something. I figured in my little mind that I would just borrow the car to run over to my great-grandmother's retirement home. She had an elevator, and I loved elevators. Besides she would enjoy seeing me. I even knew how to put the car into reverse. Too bad that the lawyer's car stopped my car from ever making it out of the parking space. Well, nothing ventured nothing gained. Dad wasn't so happy with my loving efforts to visit the rest home. Neither was the lawyer who owned the car I backed into.

My parents tell me I was a handful, always getting into trouble. My dad's favorite saying is "I only turned my head for a few seconds, and she was gone." Like the time in Hawaii, when I made it about a mile down the beach and made friends with the local stray dogs. We played on a dock until my dad found me. He then had to try and get me to go with him but the dogs wanted me to stay and play with them. Dad had to get me home without making the dogs mad. They weren't so sure that he was my real dad. Yep God gave me friends everywhere I went and my Angel was always protecting me.

Back in Wisconsin when I was about four, my parents bought a house. At that age it looked like a mansion to me. However, it held secrets that I will never forget.

Every night I would be woken up by something walking down the attic stairs and across the hall. My heart would pound and I would lay there paralyzed with fear. Unable to move or yell for my mom and dad. I would just lay there in bed and watch as this man walked into my room, crossed the floor, and would disappear into my closet. And this would happen almost every night. Soon as the apparition would walk out of sight, I would yell for my mom and dad, and they would come running.

My aunt Sherri (my mom's sister) came to live with us. She was in high school at the time. Her room was in the attic. The attic was a big room on the third floor with a winding staircase to it. My aunt would experience this man every night the same as me. However, it was from another angle. He liked to make tapping noises on the paneling in her room. He also fancied flickering the lights on and off especially on the stairs. It was a very predictable path that this man took every night. So as soon as the noises would start my aunt would sneak down the stairs and hide under my bed until he disappeared into my closet. I was so happy that I didn't have to call for my mom and dad anymore since as soon as the man went into my closet she would get into bed with me and I could sleep knowing she there. I don't think my aunt ever knew how comforting it was to have her there with me. God always sent me someone when I needed them.

At the age of five, we moved to California. Away from the cold, ice and snow. The idea of the move didn't faze me much. It was just another adventure. My brother, however wasn't very excited to start a new adventure.

I remember finding my brother crying in the alley. He was sitting against the neighbor's garage door. He had a bloody nose which he often had. I remember asking him what happened to his nose and he told me the boys down the street had hit him. Well, I loved my brother very much and went to settle the score for him. Those boys never saw me coming.

One day I was walking home from school and I had taken my aunts music box for show and tell. It was a plastic square clear with dried flowers in it. I got to the corner by the schoolyard and met up with a couple of really mean older kids. They started to push me around as I waited to cross the street. I just ignored their silliness, but one of them pushed me right out in front of a car. Luckily the driver saw what was going on and was driving very slow. Me being me I calmly got up off the ground and crossed the street with the boys laughing and making fun of me. I had made it to the opposite corner when they started to push me again. They were apparently mad about a five-year-old beating up on their two friends the other day and had to set it straight. However, I got crazy mad and yelled for them to stop or they would regret it. Well, they didn't heed the warning, and so I lifted my book bag and started spinning and letting my book bag fly with that hard plastic music box in it swing freely into the boys faces. The boys ran home crying to their mama. Their mom marched right over to our house and told my mom what I had done. Oh well, they learned their lesson that day I can assure you. I got yelled at by my mom and dad for hurting the boys and sent to my room. But boy it was worth it. I never did tell my parents they almost got me run over because in my mind it didn't matter. I solved the problem by myself, and the bit of trouble I got into was well worth it.

I don't remember much about the move to California. I know that my dad went ahead of us and drove out to find or start work. My aunt, mom, brother and I flew there.

We stayed with my dad's best friend for months in Milpitas. I made friends, and all was well for me.

One day my aunt went to school and never came home. My parents were scared to death. They contacted the police and called her friends. Days later my mom found out that my aunt had gotten into a truck with someone who drove her to Los Angeles. She was eventually picked up by the police and sent back to Wisconsin. Boy were they mad. However, for me it meant I got her bed. I was sleeping a lot better since the move because I never had to see that man in the middle of the night cross my room and enter my closet ever again.

I made a friend in the apartment complex named Jill. She lived with her mom and her 17-year-old brother. It was a bad time in my life. But I know now God was always there. He has given me the gift to handle trauma and to move on. You see Jill's 17-year-old brother told me one day when I knocked on their door that Jill couldn't play with me anymore unless I did something for him. Poor Jill, she was sitting on the staircase crying. Me being almost six had no problem doing for others. So I told him I would.

However, this was a mistake that I would never understand in all my years. It started with him telling Jill and me that we needed to kiss each other in front of him. Well, it was a game to us, so we did it and giggled. He told us to go upstairs and practice kissing. To us, it wasn't sexual it was goofing around like the grown-ups. After he would ask us to show him what we learned, we would show him, and he would let us go off to the park and play. This went on for about a week or so. He then told us we had to practice touching each other. We were still playing a game as far as we knew, We were playing adults. We did as he said and after a bit, he would have us come back downstairs and show him what we learned. He would then let us go play at the park. The park was such a fun place for us kids; we would play pirate, school, and king of the big toy. It was an after-school place to gather and play.

Jill's brother, after a week or so, started taking us into his room. He would put us in the closet and pop out the little round handle thing. I don't remember what was said or anything, but I remember him sticking his "Freddy" through the hole and making us play with it. It was a dirty adult game and a secret. However, at this point, I started to become distant. The whole thing was beginning to seem dirty and wrong. It got worse and worse. I don't remember the course it took to the fullest because God has shielded me from the pain and anguish all these years, and I thank him for that. Eventually, I stopped playing with Jill. I think she understood why. I don't remember making the conscious decision about it; God and my Angel took over when the situation started to mentally bring me down a path I was not mentally capable of handling. They removed me from this and gave me other options for playing.

I kept myself busy by the usual means of acting out my anger at what had happened. I started a grass fire in the field next to the apartments. I went into an old lady's backyard and tore up her trash and made an absolute mess. I got caught and was forced to clean it up, and dad pretty much grounded me for like forever.

Eventually, my parents bought a house in San Jose about fifteen minutes away from the apartments. I started school immediately. I don't remember the move, or anything just the little tags on the furniture from the moving company in Wisconsin.

I remember being shy, and protective of myself about making friends after the whole Jill thing. The kids in California seemed very different from back home. Their clothes and the way they talked was very different at first.

My brother and I wore a lot of hand me downs and second-hand stuff. That never bothered us until it was apparent that it was a problem for the other kids. They all wore new expensive clothes all the time, but we didn't. My parents were pretty smart. Our clothing was practical and lasting .... And lasting and lasting. And the fact that had not an ounce of style in me ever didn't help. Other kids might of been able to put something really snappy together with my clothes, but it just didn't seem necessary for me. Ultimately they made fun of me; I started to get yelled at by the teacher. Treated as if I was less than the others.

My kindergarten teacher was a nasty old woman. She was very mean most of the time. I remember a kid in our class named Trey. Trey had some mental problems. On top of that both his parents were killed in a car accident. I remember he loved to color and loved the feel of the cool crayon wax against his skin. Sort of like feathers we flutter across our skin. It wasn't something wrong or indecent; I mean other kids were putting their crayons up their noses and coloring on their teeth and eating glue. Trey just would rest the cool paperless crayon on his cheek.

One day the teacher was in a particularly bad mood and saw Trey holding a crayon to his cheek. She stomped over to him and started yelling, "So you want to color your face and be a clown then here let me help you." She proceeded to draw on his face with his crayons. Painting his face up like a clown, I felt so sad for him and angry at her for it. And anyone who has tried to write on their face with crayon knows you have to press pretty hard to get it on the skin.

Poor Trey was crying. He didn't understand why she was doing it. It hurt me just to see this happen to him. But I was five and getting in trouble was a serious problem and scary, besides I didn't want her to do that to me. I tried to befriend Trey and hang out with him during recess, but he was more content to be alone. He was always so sad, and to this day I feel for that little boy who was going through so much and treated so wrongly.

God gave me a unique in Trey. He showed me the cruelty of people, and yet he gave me the gift of compassion. I always wonder what ever happened to Trey. I never really knew if he had mental problems like autism or if he was just having a hard time with the death of his parents. Whatever the case may have been I somehow poured my love on him unknowingly with the help of my Angel. I can only hope it made some difference for him.

We did play together later that year more often than not. He was unquestionably different, but I didn't mind, I didn't see any differences between me and him. He was fun when we would play, and he would smile and laugh. That made me the happiest about being with him. I loved sharing my love with him when he was so down all the time.

The year finished, and the summer was uneventful. It was still a day and age when kids of all ages knew to stay out of the streets and out of trouble but could wander freely.

My dad had a very loud whistle, and so when it was time to go in, he would whistle, and my brother and I would come home immediately. That summer I had friends, and we all played from sunup to sundown. I even made friends with my neighbors. Diana became my best friend surprisingly fast. Her father was the neatest dad and he was very tall to me. Once he made an immense rocking ride, I don't remember why he built it. But it had these places where you climbed in and laid on the platforms that he had covered with carpet, and it would rock back and forth but never turn over. Wow, we loved that thing. It took up the whole driveway it was so big. I bet it could have fit ten kids at a time in it. Oh, the memories.

Diana was a different cookie to be sure. Her mom would have garage sales, and Nadine would put out her stuff to sell. She would put a price of $5 to $20 on beat up little trinkets. She was sure proud of her stuff. And she had very long hair that she wore in braided pony-tails every day. The good Lord taught me patience with her that year.   She was a perfectionist, in an uppity way. You know the person whose stuff is much better than anyone else. She was hard to get along with at times, but most of the time we were attached.

Diana went camping with us once, and her hair started to knot up in the braids. I thought to myself, "how hard could it be to brush it out." Oh my, her hair was so long and tangled even in the braids that I gave up brushing half-way through. We had many good times till she moved away never to be heard from again.

Our other neighbor Tom was an entirely different story. He was a very naughty kid. He dropped out of school in the 7th grade. And that's no joke, he did. However, we all played together happily for years. I even fancied myself in love with him at one point, but thankfully God had much better plans for me.

One day Tom was in a very dark mood as he sometimes got in. I don't remember why but he chased me to Diana's house next door. She wasn't home at the time, so I ran into her backyard to hide. Because when Tom was on his rampage, everyone ran and hid because he had no stop button in his brain as far as hurting someone. He chased me

to Diana's backyard and held the gate
closed so I couldn't leave. After a bit I had
had enough of his bad mood and reached
for the latch. Somehow my ring finger got
caught in the metal lock, and he pushed
the latch-up from the other side of the
fence as hard as he could. I remember the
pain and the blood. He kept it there
squeezed down on my finger for long
enough that I started to scream and hit
him over the fence. I guess he got scared
because he ran off. My finger was bleeding
and black and blue from the metal of the
lock. I even have the scar still to this day.
I think that, with the help
of God and my Angel I survived that kid. I
seriously think he would have killed
anyone of us just to see what it was like to
watch someone die. God made me pretty
resilient when it came to conflict it was
another gift he blessed me with during my
childhood.
Tom never did go back
to school and I don't think he even got a
GED. Last I heard, he was in prison for
shaking his baby till it had brain damage.
Unfortunately, Tom's parents were not
parents at all. The kids got their own
food, never showered or cleaned house. I
remember there were piles and piles of
stuff everywhere. It was an adventure
just to hang out in his room because you
had to literally climb to get down the
hallway. Thanks to Tom and my brother I
became a smoker at age 11. My mom
smoked, so it was easy to steal cigarettes
from her.

My brother gave me
three or four cigarettes and told me to
walk around the block, and when I could
smoke them without coughing I could
hang out with them, so I did. My time
growing up with Tom was a lesson to
behold.
I grew in my love for
animals because of watching Tom put his
little-matted dog into a cardboard box and
throw it across the room over and over.
Him and my brother thought that was
such fun. Why would someone even
remotely think that was fun? I can now
see how blessed I was to have chores
every day and how everyone in the house
was doing a little something made things
run smoothly. In Tom's home, it was
nothing but disrespect, screaming, and
chaos all the time. Being in his house
made me afraid all the time. It was an
unsafe environment. I think my parents
knew that and I thank God that they let
me figure it out myself. If they had said I
wasn't allowed to play over there
anymore, I would have made it a point to
disobey them. I think this would have led
me down a path of drugs, alcoholism or
prison.
One summer when I was
a teenager, the final thing that scared me
straight was the night Tom, and a few
friends went on a beer run. Well, I didn't
know that it meant to grab the beer from
the store and run. I didn't grab the beer
but man oh man I ran, far away from Tom.
I never really hung around him after that.
My brother did, they were besties for

many years even after high school. At that time my brother felt Tom could do no wrong.

The next year brought hardships of all kinds. It was a downward spiral for me and a very trying time. I was now in second grade. I like my teacher and she was a lot better than my first-grade teacher I can assure you. But I remember my hell started that year with Tamara, what a pain in the butt she was. Tamara was a child modeled, and to me, she wasn't that great looking. She started making fun of me all the time and passing me ugly notes about my hair and clothes. I remember we had to write our spelling words into sentences. I used her name in all my sentences and made sure they were not particularly nice sentences.

I had two friends, Krissy and Patty, who lived on the same block just the other side of the street. But towards the end of second-grade things changed. Both boys and girls together started pushing me around. Patty and I had gotten into an argument and I became enemy number one for her. She tormented me in school and out.

Every day on the way home from school, Patty would laugh at me, push me, tease me and when she felt like it, she would beat me up show off to the other kids. I took it, I brushed off and walked on. I was very passive with confrontations. I started to feel undeserving of friends. I would make up stories to try and get kids to like me, of course, it never worked. I couldn't sleep at night.   I had nightmares all the time. I started to nap in the afternoons after school. I had anxiety issues every day. I feared to go to class, and what hell Patty would put me through that day. I couldn't play at recess because she would torment me or beat me up. I hide in the bushes at school until I thought Patty was gone. And then would run home, as fast as I could to avoid her. Most days she was right there waiting no matter how long I hid from her.

Eventually, other kids started to get in on the action. I know now that because God made me so passive that they took that as a weakness and ganged up on me. But things got worse during the summer. I know this because I remember bits and pieces of it. The fear, the loneliness, the hurt and the mental anguish. I am still shocked, that I didn't go mental on everyone or what we use to say going postal. I tried to fight back, at first, but it would just make things so much more worse for me. I became numb, I didn't feel getting hit after a while. I even just started to let it happen to get it over with.

That summer I stayed to myself. I walked blocks and blocks to the high school to swim for 50 cents a day. It's pretty much all I did that summer. My dad would take me to the reservoir to swim for fun. However, I hate water, so I kept myself busy other ways like collecting tadpoles. I spent a lot of time at home. My favorite was when my Uncle Mark and his shipmates from the Navy would come home for the weekends. They treated me like a princess. I loved to be their center of attention. They would party the nights away and get back to the house and pass out all over the living room and family room. They could sleep through a hurricane, and I know cause my mom did some funny stuff every Saturday morning to them while they slept. But it was all in good humor.

One time mom painted one of the sailors toenails and fingernails. Poor guy didn't even realize it till he was back on the ship and in the shower days later. My brother and mom would put makeup on them, my dad always referred to makeup as war paint so mom would paint them up like Indians. It was such great fun when the sailors were home. They would drink and play cards till all hours of the morning. Dad loved playing cards it was their favorite pastime to do. I remember my Uncle Kris was in town visiting and the sailors were all there. They drank and played the card game Toledo. Anyone, who knows the game knows it's a growing pot of money. But they all were so drunk and having fun that they wouldn't realize they were broke till the next morning. My brother would get in on the action as soon as he saw them drunk enough and would win like crazy. But only in the small-time card games was he allowed to play.

I realize now that God brought those sailors into my life to give me some peace and happiness. We all did so much together over those few years they were in my life, they were constants when loneliness and heartbreak ruled my life. I think that God put them in my life to keep me balanced between good and evil. I am thankful for those memories and that time. I hope that they know how special they were to me.

Third grade was hell on earth literally for me. I was tormented every day. Even though I was only eight or nine, I contemplated suicide often. My life had become a living hell. Third grade was so bad that God granted me the ability to block out the days and just drift. I remember being petrified daily to leave the classroom.

I was threatened daily by Patty. She would pass notes to me telling me that she was going to end my life at recess. A lot of days I did wish she would. I was humiliated by her and others. Things were so bad that I would fake being sick to go to the nurse's office. I even remember picking my nose till it bled so I could get out of class.

My parents both worked and worked hard. My brother and I went to school on our own and came home on our own. I think things escalated because my brother would never get the same treatment, he would join in the "fun" publicly humiliating me. He would trip me, push me down and say such nasty mean things to me in front of everybody whether at school or home. His treatment of me was his ticket out of being treated the same. So instead of standing up for me as I had for him back in Wisconsin, he joined in on the torment. I had no protectors and no friends. I resigned myself to this being what life was going to be for me.

Growing up all I wanted from my brother was a little attention, Whether it be positive or negative. I wanted him to love me, and to show it. I would have died for him to give me an ounce of kindness. Unfortunately he never really did.

All the way through elementary I was a punching bag for all the kids and teachers. Yes, and there were teachers that didn't care about us kids. They used me to find new ways of humiliation. However, not all were like that. A lot of them just stayed out of it and went about their business. Bullies were a part of life then, and you either stood up for yourself or shut up and waited in the corner.

Sometimes some kids would let me play with them. They would let me jump rope with them so they could trip me with the rope or hit me with it for their amusement. They would allow me to play ball with them so they could try and knock me in the face with it or trip me on bases. It was also great fun to hit me with the tetherball in the face that was always worth a lot of points.

Patty made sure I wasn't allowed to use the bathroom or fountains. She took my lunch money from me daily, and I would have to go without lunch or take the chance of my parents finding out

I was so hated. I hated recess, and I hated free time.

Everything changed for me in the fifth grade. My new teacher, Mrs. Miller, was outstanding. She treated me kindly and gave me protection and understanding from the other kids. In her class, I wasn't afraid because when someone would make a hostile remark to me, she would reprimand them immediately. That year everyone except Patty, of course, left me alone. However, that was also the year my only friend at the time died.

There was a girl named Andrea. She was a lot like me in her treatment from the other kids. I was never the only one bullied there were several of us who other kids deemed unworthy of their friendship or kindness. Andrea had Cystic Fibrosis and missed a lot of school. She was made fun of and tormented as I was.   She was small for her age and always pale white. She sat out all the time since she was too sick to run around. She and I became friends that year even though she was in sixth grade. I would never wait for her at recess because I was afraid that she would turn on me and reject me, so I let her come to me.

For months things went great. Andrea was a huge fan of Rick Springfield after all it was the early 80's. She had lots of videos of him, and we would go to her house after school and

just sit and watch them. However one-day
things changed between us. Andrea
became sick, a lot frailer than usual. She
was on oxygen all the time, and she rarely
attended school. She often talked about
how she was going to die soon, and it
didn't seem to faze her, it was accepted,
by her and her parents. At least that's
what it appeared like to me.

One day when she hadn't
been at the school for a while, I went to
her house to check up on her. When she
was sick, her mom or dad was usually
home with her and sent me away (but not
in a mean way). This time she was home
alone. She seemed happy to see me and
let me in. She always coughed a lot, but
this time it was a deep and unrelenting.
We watched Rick Springfield videos on
VHS for a little while then all of a sudden
she jumped up, ran into the kitchen, and
grabbed a knife and started yelling at me
that she was going to cut me up and kill
me. At first, I thought she was joking. But
the look in her eyes told me instinctively
that some switch happened in that
second. She chased me into the backyard
swinging her knife and trying so hard to
stab me. She was very slow and just
slashing the knife in every direction. I ran
for the side gate and ran all the way home.
A week later she was back in school and
was waiting for me outside my class. She
asked me to come over to her house after
school and acted like nothing was amiss. I
walked home with her, and as soon as we
got into her house, she grabbed a knife
and chased me out the back door again,

screaming and yelling that I was going to die. In my heart, I knew that God wanted me to go back, so I did for a few weeks. Some days I ran for my life others were just ordinary. Andrea fell sick again, and she was gone a long time from school. The times I went to her house her mom said she was too sick to play. After about three weeks of her being gone, I went to her house, and her mom answered the door. I asked if Andrea could play today and her mother just looked at me sadly and said, "oh honey she died, she isn't here anymore." I went home in a daze and never got to say goodbye. I can understand from that experience that its hard to have some kind of closer when you don't have a body or are present when someone passes. It was hard to believe back.she was gone because one day she was there the next she was not.

Some may think that I kept going back because she was my only friend. But the truth is, I loved her as a sister in God, I had compassion for her, and my heart ached every time she would "cough up a lung" as she would say. I realize now that God and her and my Angel all knew she needed that friendship towards the end. I didn't know she would die, I mean, in my world people didn't die unless they were old. Now that I look back I also knew that she did want to kill me. Not because she was psycho but because she was scared to die. She just didn't want to go alone. She feared death; she probably wanted to see death before she had to go through it.

God gives us trials and tribulations, our openness and love for God will determine the outcome of hardships. He infused me with his love and gave me protection when I needed it even if I didn't know at the time. God and Angel were always with me in every instance and helped me to move on or stand up, shake off and or take on the next hardship. God made me strong and gave me many abilities to deal with life at the time. It's correct that kids can be cruel and mean hearted. If they would listen to God and their Angel this world would be a much happier place.

I drifted through elementary school, and I don't remember much of it. However, I do not hold any grudge towards anyone, because it is not my place to do so, God won't be asking me about their sins he will ask me about my own. And who we are as kids does not define us as adults. People can change at any point in their lives for good or bad.

The once cruel and mouthy kid can become a pastor or a doctor or maybe a missionary.

Pebbles can turn into stones which can turn into boulders and eventually into mountains. But with God, and our love for each other we can move mountains with our faith. I don't see the boulders in my path, all I see is a path I need to take. My faith will guide me and my love, and my Angel will light the way.

Everyone will have boulders or mountains to cross. The question is will you carry on alone or with the love of God.

I choose to leave the bullies in the past and forgive. That is a gift, and it's a gift we all need to learn to give and to receive. Holding onto all that hate would have made me a very bitter person in the end. I don't think that is what God would want for any of us. If I came across any of these kids I probably wouldn't know them if I saw them. But If I came face to face with them I would treat them as I do any other person. I don't need apologies from anyone, it is what it was. It's done and over, let us forgive forget and move on.

I would rather live each day as if there was a God and die to find out there isn't than live each day as if there was no God and find out there is.

Author

Unknown

Chapter 2

My Angel

You will hear me referring to My Angel throughout these short chapters. My Angel is a big part of my spiritual life here on earth. I haven't had the pleasure of being told my Angel's name, but I know without a doubt my Angel is there to help and guide me. My Angel helps me reason my way through life. Helps me make good choices, although I don't always listen. And someday my Angel will gently and lovingly take me back to heaven. His job is to guide me, lead me, and protect my soul.

You see there *ARE* Angels. Everyone has an Angel from the moment you are born until you are safely back home with God. Your Angel loves you, adores you and no matter what will never leave you for one second.

Angels are one of God's greatest gifts. See we possess a piece of God in each one of us. We are eternally part of God. And God thinks we are pretty precious and gives us each at least one Angel to protect our souls, our piece of heaven itself is in each of us. Only we are made in God's image. And for that reason, our Angels love us more than any human could love another human. I have read that Angels are neither male nor female. But for this case, I will refer to my Angel as he.

I do not have to prove anything to him as I do not have to prove anything to God nor do they have to prove anything to me. It is richly ingrained in me the belief of God and my Angel as well as your Angel, that this knowledge is as real and genuine to me as the sky itself. The sky IS blue that is a fact, My God and my Angel ARE real, and that's a fact.

You or no-other will ever be able to change my mind about them. My faith maybe great, but I can waver, after all I am human. My faith is tested daily, and I fail on many occasions. But even though I may fail the test my faith will not fail. I will make wrong decisions, and I will sin. It's just simple as that. To accept this is to accept that you are human. You have a little speck of God, however you are not God.

During those years of torment, it was my Angel whispering in my ear "God loves you", "I love you, and you are not alone". Did I always listen? Of course not, we are children of God, not

Jesus. God gave us freewill to choose good or bad. Our choice determines the outcome of that path. Your parents wouldn't let you go into the wolf's den alone, would they? Well, I hope they wouldn't. Well God didn't send you here to this earth to go it alone either. He entrusted your soul to the capable hands of your Angel. And there are more Angels at your beckon call if you ask. God tells us He will send Angels, and I don't think He was lying. When you pray, they pray when you cry, they cry, when you love someone they love too. I bet when you dress up for Halloween they dress up too.

The "unconditional love" is what they feel for you. So talk to your Angel. You don't have to know your Angel's name. Make one up, they won't care what you call them as long as you call on them to do God's will. Because that's what we strive to do, God's will and they help us do that.

They are that voice that tells you to stay home today. Or to hug that stranger or give a thumbs up to someone. You may never know the outcome of your action, but there will be something that your love does for someone else. Everything your Angel does for you is for the love of God.

There is life beyond this one. There is also life within this one. There is a war going on all around us for our souls. Angels and Demons always going at it for the prize. I believe that some people, when they die, are afraid to go on. Maybe it's an unknown to them and that scares them. It is still a part of our freewill to go to heaven. So some get stuck here and then we get hauntings. But I believe all spirits can move on at any time, God's house is always open to his children. He always leaves the porch light on.

However, I also believe that evil spirits are afoot all the time. See when God cast them out of heaven, He made sure they had no part of him in them.   Therefore, removing that person from his presence.

I can't believe that we come from nothing and that there isn't some kind of order to the madness. We have to make the spiritual connection to God as well as the religious connection. The things that we as humans are veiled from like the eternal war of good vs. evil. Sometimes things break through that vail and we can catch a glimpse into the spirit world. Just my feelings on the subject.

For He orders His Angels to protect you wherever you go. They will hold you with their hands to keep you from striking

your foot on a stone. They
will trample down lions and
poisonous snakes, crush
fierce lions and serpents
under your feet.

Psalm 91:11 - 13

But Angels are
only servants. They are
spirits sent from God to
care for those who will
receive salvation.

Hebrews 1:14

Chapter 3

Accident from God

Now my brother isn't the nicest of people I will say. He is mean and selfish for all that's worth. But people can change and he is still on my prayer list for that. However, he played a significant part in a lot of the battles I face going through my adult life. My brother never hugged me, and I don't recall him ever saying I love you. He never stood up for me or protected me. My brother has had a dislike for me since the day I was born. Don't get me wrong I do not blame him for anything. His and others actions played a vital role in making me who I am today. And for that I am thankful.

I love my brother. I love him to the moon and back and will till the day I die. However, he has cast me out of his life, and that was his choice, not mine.

However one of the most important incidents in my life was when I was 17 and I adored the ground my brother walked on. I went to visit him in Los Angeles for a few days on my way to visit a friend in Arizona. My aunt was going from California to Arizona to visit her friends and my other aunt. On the way, she was stopping for a few days in Los Angeles, and I rode along. She dropped me off at my one of my other Aunt's house where my brother and his roommate picked me up. As a surprise, my loving brother took me to the bar they frequented often. Was he doing this for me? No! I was there and they wanted to go to the bar, so I had to go. Oh and yes I was underage seventeen in fact, and the bartender served me alcohol. But man was I sitting on the high horse.

After getting so drunk that we couldn't see straight, my brother and his roommate, Carl, decided it was time to go. They walked over to Carl's little Honda Civic, and I panicked. I was so drunk I felt nothing. But at the same time I still had the good sense to know we needed to call a cab. My brother Bobby jumped up on the roof of the car and started yelling I will surf home! I stood there not getting in the car. Again my Angel was warning me against this choice to get in the car. I was listening for the most part. I pleaded with Bobby to call a cab. Told him I would pay for it.

"Awww we do this all the time, practically every night nothing will happen we only live down the street, I promise." Yeah well I should've known better than to believe any promise he made. Against my better judgment, I got in the car. How bad could it be we are only a few miles from his apartment.

Well, I can honestly say my Angel warned me. In fact, he was probably screaming at me by this time to call a cab. And for the rest of my life, I will wish I would have listened to him.

Unfortunately, I was so drunk that it's all I could do to keep from passing out in the back seat of this tiny death trap I was now stuck in.

We headed to the apartment and turned on the main road with my brother and Carl just laughing and singing. I took my shoes off in the back seat and laid against the little window. I remember I was wearing a red mini skirt high heel boots and nylons.

We were cruising along when Roy and my brother started to sing the Weebles song. You know Weebles wobble, but they don't fall down. Then Roy started swaying the little car back and forth along with the song, just singing along. However, he sped up for the next turn and continued to play Weebles. Roy ended up hitting the corner at about 60 miles an hour, and we were to turn right onto Sunset Blvd. But he was too drunk and going too fast. He lost control, the wheels buckled and we ended up on the wrong side of the road. To compensate Roy tried to turn the car towards the right side of the road. Guess he didn't see the big median in the middle with the trees and cement curbs. The little vehicle jumped, turned and maybe even rolled. Next thing I knew we were staring at a brick wall.

I couldn't breathe and I was gasping for breath trying to refill my lungs. I had enough sense to realize that the air had been knocked from my lungs. So I attempted to stay calm and remember to take deep breaths and oh how it hurt so bad. My brother came too and jumped out of the car yelling at me to get out and run. In a panic, I climbed out of the car as my brother threw me his keys and told me to go down two stop lights and turn left. So I ran, barefooted and for all I was worth, I just ran before the police would arrive. My brother told me that if I were caught, he would go to jail and he and the bar would be in trouble. I wasn't hurting anywhere except my lungs, so I ran. But I was injured and seriously, but the shock of everything kept me from feeling any pain, I could only react at this time.

I heard the sirens coming in the distance, so I ran harder and farther. The accident sobered me up real quick. But I was in an unfamiliar town, in a strange area, in the middle of the night. So I stopped and listened, I couldn't hear the sirens anymore. But I saw a police car coming down the road and I ducked into a parking garage and sat between 2 parked cars. Next thing I remember a security guard was honking at me. I told him I had a fight with my boyfriend outside an Italian restaurant, at the big mall and that

I needed to call a cab. I WAS lost, I was panicking, and I had just realized that I passed out between two cars in a parking lot in the middle of the night.

I guess I was out for at least an hour because the guard said he thought he saw me sitting there earlier but didn't get a good look and thought his eyes were playing tricks on him. It bugged him for about an hour before he decided to go back and look again. And by that time I was coming to. Still no pain and no sense anything was even wrong with my body.

We went over to the restaurant that was now closed and locked. However, the manager was still in there counting money. He let me in, and I called a cab. The security guard stayed with me asking questions while I waited for the cab.

I told him my boyfriend and I got into a fight and I had already taken my shoes off in his car when he kicked me out of it. He said that it must have been while the vehicle was still moving from the state I was in. He knew something was up and probably knew I was lying about something. You have to admit it was a good storyline on the spur of the moment.

The cab arrived, and the security guard told me to take care of myself. He was undoubtedly concerned about the state I was in. I then gave the driver my brothers address, that I knew by heart from writing him all the time and he drove me to the apartment complex.

He offered to walk me to the door. I refused the help politely. I did know my way around his apartment complex, so that was a plus.

After making it to the apartment, I plopped down on the couch. I must've passed out again because the sun was coming up and two of my brother's friends walked into the apartment and looked freaked out. They said they had been sent there to find me and take me to my brother at the hospital. I told them I would just change clothes and go with them. I did know them from other visits, so I knew I was safe.

It was then that I realized my suitcase was in the car still and that it was no doubt towed to a yard. I grabbed a pair of sweatpants from my brother's room and headed out to the hospital with the two friends. I don't remember much more, except that because they saw me in the emergency room as a family member, they let me see Carl who was in a coma, and his face was tore up and swollen. I'm pretty sure my Angel got me in there to show me what could have happened to me, you know a scare tactic. After seeing Carl's I went to my brother's room, He was dressing, and I saw he had a big long streaking bruise across his chest. He was the only one smart enough to wear a seatbelt. I guess it was self-preservation that made him buckle up. Or he listened to his Angel. I don't remember anything else from LA really except that Carl was discharged from the hospital and he swore he would never drink again. But he decided to grab a six-pack of beer on the way home. When he got there, he took several pills and passed out on the couch.

At one point my Aunt came looking for me, and my brother locked the door and told me to pretend nobody was home so she would go away. He was buying time since my suitcase was still in the car. Later that day, a few days after the accident Roy and Bobby went to look at the car. The officer told them at the yard that they were lucky to be alive. The Honda was the fifth car to crash into that very spot in the wall, but we were the first to survive.

My brother retrieved my suitcase, and I finally got to change clothes. I still had no real pain just a massive headache and I slept most of the time I was there. My aunt came and got me, and we headed to Arizona as though nothing happened. Unfortunately, my suitcase that I borrowed from my dad had a gigantic hole in it and was scraped up all over. My brother and I told my aunt that I had fallen down the flight of stairs leading to his second-floor apartment. I was limping but didn't know why, so this gave an excuse for any suspicions she might have had.

I slept the whole way to Arizona. By the time we arrived and got to my Aunt's house I was hurting pretty bad on my lower legs and ankles. My legs had scratches down the front of both of them, but I still saw no real bruising or anything until I took off my shoes. My legs, ankles and feet were swollen so bad that my pants were tight around that part of my leg. I still felt no real pain.

The rest of the trip was pretty much a blur, I went to my friend Sue's and I remember watching MTV, and it had flashed that Stevie Ray Vaughan had died. I fell asleep at my friend's house in a recliner, she woke me up in a panic and told me I had been sleeping for two days. I don't remember anything else from that trip.

Back in California after my almost deadly trip, I started having severe headaches in the back of my head. And my neck always hurt and was stiff, and my legs were black and blue. My ankles were one pure nasty bruise and on my left outer thigh was a bruise the size of a football. It had been almost two weeks since the accident.

I told my mom and dad that I had fallen down the stairs at Bobby's apartment and that these things were a result of it. Because of the problems I was having and the pain, I was starting to get worried about what was wrong with me. My mom sent me to Dr. Sunshine (yes that was her real name). I told the Dr. my little lie about the stairs. She had X-rays taken of my whole body. When she came back in the room, she was shaking her head. She said that I had a three-inch break in the back of my skull. She said I was lucky to be alive since I didn't get medical attention right away. The doctor told me that I was suffering from a concussion and unfortunately, the

lasting effects could only be determined
with time.

Dr. Sunshine explained
to me that I was sleeping so much because
of the concussion I had and I was lucky
that I woke up at all. She examined my
head with a flashlight and told me that
whole back of my head was still slightly
swollen and bruised. But that wasn't all
she found. Both my ankles had hairline
fractures. The doctor also did a test on my
shins with a small instrument that had
pointed needles on it.

She ran it up and down the
front of my shins and found that I had no
feeling anywhere on them. Both my
wrists had hairline fractures. The doctor
told me that it must have been some stairs
I feel down. I couldn't lie to her anymore,
so I broke down and told her the truth. I
was feeling so blessed that I had lived
through it, even though I might not have
thought of it that way at the time.

She told me that it was
too late for any preventative measures for
my skull fracture. She said I woke up and
that was the one good thing out of this
whole situation. Dr. Sunshine stated that
it was possible that if my friend hadn't
woken me up, that I might be in a coma
and may have never woke again.

Well, I am in my forties
now, and the lasting effects have slowly
become clear over the years.

Because I chose not to
listen to my Angel or my my own good
sence that night, I now have a memory
loss issue. I don't remember a lot of

things from minute to minute. This drives my husband crazy, and others insane as well as entertains people. I get yelled a lot from people for forgetting something just told me. I can forget the first part of the question before you finish. Someone can ask me to do something and I walk into the next room and have already forgotten what I was supposed to do. I can drive and not remember parts of the trip. My memory is beyond aging memory problems it's like I keep losing information from the time of the accident and it never really stops.

I have learned that my memory isn't going to get better so I will deal with it day by day. And that means everyone else can just deal with it. When people get mad at me for forgetting, I say to myself, "God gave me this gift for whatever reason and I will embrace it". Some might say I am being disciplined for making such bad choices. Truth is I went down that road of thought a time or two. I have come to learn that I made a wrong decision, in fact, I have made several in my life as I am sure you have. This was a learning experience for mind body and soul. I am thankful to be alive and grateful for all that came with this event. It sobered me up. I had a new perspective of the outcomes of my decisions. I became more aware of the after effects of thing that I do.

I have always felt that God gave all of us the gift of freewill. That's one main reason He sent us here with Angels to help. We are human and we make mistakes. If you didn't make mistakes or error, then you would be Jesus.

My inability to remember is a constant reminder how one wrong choice could have cost me my life before my time. My loss of memory is a gift I can forget things too quickly but some of the things I need to forget. My memory problem doesn't stop me from remembering all things. It just hinders my memory process. It's not something I can explain outright.

But let me try it this way. Most people will hold onto memories and let them eat away at them. People will remember all the bad things someone did to them. Some memories will cause guilty feelings or anger after dwelling on them. I may remember something about it, but all the emotions and rage is genuinely forgotten.

The other effect is I don't process information quickly. I can give a complete heartfelt answer, but I will need to think about it for a minute before I answer that is if I remember what you were asking me. If someone yells at me, I won't come up with a snappy comeback until after you have long left the conversation. What I hear doesn't always process to my brain. In a way, I'm impaired because I don't regularly make the connection of what someone says, from what I hear and to what my brain will process. That's the only way I know how to describe it. In the accident

something was damaged, something in
my head that processes information.
Why would this be a
blessing? Well, that's pretty easy to
explain. I don't have a quick wit, and I am
not prone to make snappy judgments
about people. In fact, in accepting my
limitations I have learned more with
them, then I would have without. I'm not
handicap per say, and I still live a full and
blessed life. No one person can do
everything or be blessed with every gift.
There is a limit to our human abilities
because we would never need anyone else
in our lives. We have to have limitations,
or we will never need the divine
knowledge or help that God and the
Angels and other people can add to our
life experiences.
It's true that in this life
we can do and be anything we wish to do
or be. But why would one want to?
Personally, I think it is more fulfilling to
accomplish what God sets before me. And
to look back and see what I have done for
Him in my lifetime, and tell others what
He has done for me.

Chapter 4

When the Lord Calls on You

Have you ever had that nagging feeling to give that homeless person a dollar? And you passed on it and it still nags you hours later. Well, that's God calling on you. When God wants you to do something he will nag and nag until you do it or until the opportunity passes.

It's not always easy to understand God when He calls us to do His will. That's why it is important to let God know in your prayers that you are willing to do His will. I personally tell Him all the time that He has blessed me with memory problems, so He needs to remind me sometimes to fulfill something.

If you're in line at a stop light and you see someone holding a sign "Broke down and no money, please help," you might think to yourself, "I'm not giving him a dollar because he will just get drugs with it." And yes that is true he might buy drugs with it or get drunk. However, it's not our job to judge that person or what that person will do with the dollar. You give with God's love, and that blesses that dollar. If he takes that dollar and does ill with it, then that dollar becomes cursed for that person.

God may put a blessing on that dollar and want you to give it to the man because when he buys drugs with it, he might overdose and end up in the hospital. Where in turn he may go to treatment and counseling and get his life back. All from your dollar, you didn't want to give in the first place.

God isn't going to make that dollar jump out of your purse or wallet and slap you in the face with a loud trumpet and a voice commanding you to give that dollar. God doesn't work that way, he will put it on your heart, and you are supposed to act. It's simple, you have a dollar, he is asking for a dollar, you give him the dollar and God blesses you and the dollar.

> Give to the one who begs from you, and do not refuse the one who would borrow from you.
>
> Matthew 5:42

The Bible tells us to help our neighbors, and anything asked of you by someone, if it's within your powers you do it then you should do it. God gives us everything we have. He blesses us with everything we need. You need to use these blessings of God to help others.

So what if your neighbor is mean or foul-mouthed. You still do what you can to help him.

Here is a piece of advice, Love and like are two different things. You love thy neighbor, but God doesn't say you have to like them.

If your neighbor is trying to mow his lawn and his mower breaks down, you may be blessed with the knowledge to fix it. Or you may have a mower they can use. These acts are what shows the face of God. If that person doesn't accept your help then that's on them God still blesses you for trying. Your act of kindness may be just one in many that, that person needs before he will see God in these blessings. Never underestimate God's power, his will, will be done whether it's you or someone else.

I am not an outspoken type person. I don't usually stand up for myself or argue about myself to someone. It's just not who I am, and whatever the situation happens to be I am normally silent in my own defense. This is because I don't have the wit to say everything that needs to be said. I also know that I may not be seeing the situation as it is in others eyes. I would rather just be blamed for something and let God sort it out. And on the other hand, I don't like hurting or upsetting people.

Now I'm not saying I don't ever stand up for myself. I have on occasion gotten defensive when confronted. I try to let God lead me but sometimes my emotions take over, and I can get into an argument with someone. I am by no means perfect or sinless. I am human, and I have human emotions. So I do get mad, and I do run my mouth sometimes when it should be shut.   I have frustrations and anger just like everyone else. However, I am able to forget and forgive quickly. I can love you the same after we just had it out and said nasty things to each other.

Once at my church one of the women who did charity work outside of church stood in front of our small congregation and asked the people of our church to donate paper products to a woman's shelter. Like tissues, toilet paper, and paper towels. The next week very little was brought but a pack of toilet paper. This angered me, and immediately God put on my heart to say something, that is very out of my comfort zone. I had watched for weeks people not giving in our church, and it was really pushing my buttons. So I gave it over to God, and I stood when asked if anyone had anything to announce.

I remember I didn't mince words I just wanted to say what God wanted me to say and sit down. Of course, I don't remember most of what I said, but that's ok it was God's words.

All I remember is the point was that a member of our congregation asked for the help of donations to a relevant charity and our group didn't step up. So I told them, "when someone comes to you and asks for something it's not just that person asking it's God Himself. If you don't honor that call, then you are not honoring God. Do you really want to tell God NO"!

Well, a lot of people do, even in my own small church. I have seen people all over give but with great fanfare to themselves. I have seen people put five dollars in the collection and take out change. I have seen people try to rule the church with what they wanted to happen and want others to agree whether it's right or wrong. I have seen others put people down and look down on someone who doesn't live or dress as they do. I will stand for God when He tells me to, but sometimes God tells me to let them reap what they sow. He says "let it go, Vicki, and let me do My work".

The point is if you don't act for God then you make Him sad, you will lose that blessing and the two dollars you put in the collection plate. It's not always what you give it's also the spirit of giving. For goodness sakes leave the whole five dollars in the collection and bring the dang toilet paper.

I use to teach the youth
group and children's Sunday school.
Every once in a while our kids at church
would have a fundraiser to raise money
for one reason or another. Our main thing
was a spaghetti dinner. For the longest
time, our church or I would buy the
ingredients, the kids would cook and
serve. Our turn out actually depended on
what sports team was playing during the
dinner. It was sad to put so much
planning and effort into an event and have
three people show up because a
basketball game was on at that time.
Eventually, I got the congregation to start
donating the ingredients and even
shamed some into showing up. Bad ? I
don't know, but hey it worked. Either way
if you're lead by God then you better act,
or He will hound you until you do.

Chapter 5
Dealing With Loss

Everyone has a story of losing someone. It doesn't matter what the loss is, it can cause grief in your heart. God doesn't want to see us hurt and grieve. Unfortunately, it is a part of our human nature when we say goodbye to someone who has passed. Our Angels are always there to comfort us during these times. Remember that our Angels love us and do not want us to hurt. Our grief our pain is their grief and pain.

I believe that death is a magnificent gift from God. What better gift than to be called home. Some people are more ready to go than others. As for myself, I am ready when God is. I will be sad to leave my family but happy to be home.

I do not believe a person dies unless God wills it. I have heard people ask "if there is a God why does he let bad things happen." The truth is, people let bad things happen. People do bad things to other people. Our Angels and the Angels of others will try to lead someone away from hurting another person or themselves. But again it comes down to the listening part. People don't listen to them or God and in turn beat, maim or even murder. This is not ever limited to age, beauty or species. People kill, people kill loved ones, they kill children, and they kill perfect strangers.

We have free will, and that free will determine the outcome of every path we take in life. Our free will can also alter or affect the path of others. If you murder someone, you're not just slaying them, you are hurting everyone connected to that person in one way or another. You are even affecting people that that person didn't even know.

Everyone hears about the ripple effect when you drop a pebble in the water. And that pebble forever changed that one spot where it landed. In turn, that pebble may displace a crawfish which was supposed to be dinner for a bass and so on. Or the pebble may have landed just so, and made a nice hiding spot for a little fish. The ripple effect would drive us mad thinking of every possibility that pebble could have. That's why God takes care of all that. He already knows if that fish needs shelter, He already knows everything pebble concerned will be and do. So we don't have to worry about things like that. But we still need to be aware that our actions will always have a cause and effect. Think before you act, and think before you talk.

I am confident there are many cases where God uses someone who has evil around them. Look at Judas, He wasn't evil, Judas had a purpose, and that was to betray Jesus. I don't believe he went to hell for it. I think he carried out the command of God. His path was set for him before his conception. Judas listened to God and his Angel and did what he was sent to do. If Judas had not betrayed Jesus then who would have. How would Jesus have gone to the cross for our sins if Judas had not betrayed him?   Sure someone would have, but it probably wasn't part of the plan, ripple and effect again.   Now the fact that he committed suicide because of his guilt is proof to me that he loves Jesus and only did what he was unconsciously directed to do. He was a means to an end. Jesus was part human, he knew he had to go to the cross, he didn't want to, yet he wanted to, and he begged not to. He needed help to get where he needed to go, and Judas had the hardest job of them all as far as I'm concerned.

So maybe evil helps to murder someone. If your faith is in place, then you have nothing to worry about. We need to protect every spark for God. So that we may return it to him. Our Angels will help guard that spark, but evil wants it more than we seem to want it. Don't let Satan have it! Even a murderer has that spark of God. And until he dies it still belongs to the Father that gave it. And what I mean by that is, we have our whole life to make choices and in the end either we destroy that spark of God and

give the most powerful thing in all of the
Universes to Satan, or we live happily
ever after with God.

Our loved ones with faith
are well taken care of in heaven, it's
where our souls want to be. Sometimes
our human nature and all that comes with
it sucks us into an abyss we think we can't
escape. But until our last breath, there is
hope, there is love and happiness that
awaits us.

Our loved ones don't
grieve, hurt or cry anymore. They are in
the presence of God Himself. They are
rejoicing in the glory of the All Mighty. It's
us left behind that cry, hurt and grieves
for them. And we need to remember
heaven isn't a prison and our loved ones
come and go. Once they go to heaven
their eternal soul is forever and eternally
Gods.

In 2014 my grief was so
bad. I had contemplated death and
wished for it. See, that year I found out I
was pregnant with baby number four. At
my 12-week appointment, I had an
ultrasound. She was just a kicking and a
bouncing. Lance even made a joke to the
doctor about yelling at the baby to behave
so she could get a proper heartbeat
reading. Eventually, the doctor got the
readings she needed and gave the all is
normal.

At the time I was working
in Kansas with Lance, but he was gone
pretty much permanently by this point to
Texas on another job site. We made a
choice for me to return back to Arkansas

where our support system is. Three kids at once can be a handful. I had plans to finish my Bachelor degree in teaching after the baby was born. To do that I needed help from our family to accomplish that feat. By the end of June, the kids and I were all settled back in Arkansas at home. It was a great few months for me. I reconnected with my church, and I always love that. But around the first week of July, I had missed my 16 week checkup, and my doctor was out of town for my last appointment with her. I was starting to get a bad feeling, my belly was growing like it should be. We finally found a doctor in town who would take me as his new patient, they got us in for the next day I was so excited. Never in my wildest dreams would I think anything could be wrong, I had no signs of distress, I was getting the ultrasound that would tell me whether it is a boy or girl. Sadly there was no heartbeat. On the screen, she was as still as could be. I realize now that God blessed me with that last picture of her in my mind. Her head, arms and little legs all visible. God blessed me with that picture because ordinarily I wouldn't remember it or be able to recall it vividly. But I can, and I am blessed with it and the last ultrasound forever in my memory.

We honestly didn't know if it was a boy or girl, but the human side of me has to label the baby. Lance and I gave her a name of Solaris, she was approximately 13 weeks along. I remember at that time feeling little vibrations in my belly. I even said to my nephew that it feels like she is convulsing. Unfortunately, she probably was.

The loss of Solaris broke my heart. It was a pain I wouldn't even wish on my worst enemy. I went through what I call a shutout phase. I had no desire to see or talk to anyone. I also went through the denial phase. When the doctor told me there was no heartbeat and that she stopped growing two months prior, I still denied that it was possible for her to be gone. When the doctor brought up having a D&C, I was against it because I just couldn't believe she was gone and the surgery would kill her if for some reason they had made a mistake.

I went through a lot of stages during this time. I felt that God was punishing me for all my bad mistakes I had made in my life. That to me was the only reason He would take her. Or maybe He thought me unfit to give her to, perhaps He thinks I am an unfit mother. I even blamed myself even though the doctor explained that it is a very common thing to lose a baby during those first few months. But nothing was going to soothe my pain and anguish. I was disappointed in myself, and I was disappointed and felt I had let God down.

However, after a few months, when my body and mind was getting back to normal, I started to turn to God more and more each day. I began by being mad at Him, giving Him a few good talking to's, wanting answers but my faith never really wavered I was still turning to him. I didn't turn away from Him I went

TO Him. Even psychotic as I was I still knew deep down that God had a plan, and this was part of it.

One day, I had a thought pop into my head, and I began to think a little bit. I believe full heartedly that Solaris was in heaven. Well, who do you think she was in heaven with? My family that has passed on before me, the Angels, Jesus, and God Himself. Who better to watch over her till I get there but God Himself! The perfect of perfect babysitters! After all, He created her in His own image. He loves her more than anyone else could ever imagine.

You know when your kids are mad at you for something stupid like they broke their toy and now it's your fault. But after a few minutes, the anger passes, and they are your best friend again. That's kind of how it was with God. I was so mad at Him, then I realized that she was a blessing for the short time I had her, even if she was only inside me. I believe God knew that if she were born and then died, it would have been the end of my world. I think He was protecting me in from that. It hurt to lose her while pregnant. I couldn't imagine her being born and then taken. My heart breaks even now for myself and others who have experienced the death of their child whether unborn or born.

But we do not
want you to be uninformed,
brothers, about those who
are asleep, that you may not
grieve as others do who
have no hope. For since we
believe that Jesus died and
rose again, even so, through
Jesus, God will bring with
him those who have fallen
asleep. For this we declare
to you by a word from the
Lord, that we who are alive,
who are left until the
coming of the Lord, will not
precede those who have
fallen asleep. For the Lord
himself will descend from
heaven with a cry of
command, with the voice of
an Archangel, and with the
sound of the trumpet of
God. And the dead in Christ

will rise first. Then we who are alive, who are left, will be caught up together with them in the clouds to meet the Lord in the air, and so we will always be with the Lord. ...

1 Thessalonians 4:13-18

Chapter 6

Religion of All Colors

I have been asked several times about my feelings on religion. To me, religion is pretty simple as far as worship. Most churches will let anyone come and worship with them, and this is a great thing. I believe we can worship at any church.

Kind of like this: Some
people like scary movies, then they want
to see a romance than a drama with
action. Worship is like this to me. Some
days I want to worship with hell and
brimstone preaching, some days I wish
for loving peaceful worship. And
sometimes I want the beautiful worship in
ceremonial.
I connect to God in so
many different ways. I love to talk about
Him, write about Him, most of all I love to
sing about Him, and that's when I really
connect with Him.
To me religions are like
knowledge, you have to experience
different things to learn. I can experience

so much with a song to the Lord and it brings my prayers to a whole new level of consciousness. I have been known to sing all day long, and my heart gets light, and I feel the love I am exchanging with God. Like having a parent at your very own recital and He listens with love and intensity.

You have to find the religion or denomination that best suits you. You have to connect and feel the love and energy of the worship. The churches I stay away from are the ones that say they are the only ones going to heaven. And that you have to worship the way they do and like it or you won't go to heaven.

Religion is a state of mind to me. It has labels like Catholics, Lutheran, Muslim, Presbyterian, and so on. But the truth is most all religions worship God, and I believe that the ones who are open to people not of their religion worshiping with them are the ones that are close to God. I want to worship with the Jews and see what it is like, worship with a Muslim or even a Fundamentalist Baptist. I have my beliefs and they are set in stone for myself. No matter the church I go to they cannot corrupt me or change my views. When you are connected to God you can get a feeling or the chills or whatever that says "Hey that isn't right with God".

In my heart, I believe that different religions and churches are just a different way to worship God and that's all. Everyone needs a church home. But it should be okay to visit other religions too. I think we should do a significant movement and go to other churches at least once a month to learn how they worship. If they don't welcome you with open arms then as the bible says to wipe the dust from your feet.

All religions have their issues. Priests went bad, nuns have gone rogue. Corruption at the governments of the churches, stealing and pushing politics to their own benefit. No preacher or congregation should judge you or tell you, you are bad.

If you go to a church and you don't like the feeling you get then get out, or speak up and ask questions. Your pastor should be kind and listen to you and help you anyway he can. Your church shouldn't feel like a cult or a club you have to join to be a part of. It should be like coming home to family. A place to find help and love.

Sometimes, unfortunately religions are used to further political careers or wars. Some people may feel safer with a leader who they think is religious. I however feel safer with someone who practices and openly worships.

IF a religion promises to give you something other than eternal salvation for your devotion then it's time to look at that religion. You know ones that say, if you blow up innocent people then there will be women waiting for you in Heaven. I have never read anything in the bible to insinuate that God was a pimp of any kind. And if God was keeping virgin women aside for the pleasure of these men then what about the virgin women? Who are they and why would God punish them? I think that the view of virgins awaiting a man in heaven is just ridiculous to say the least. And to even suggest that a heinous crime would get you some reward in heaven is just silly to believe. However God will forgive the dirtiest of sinners and wash them clean, as long as they know they have sinned and repent.

God welcomes all sinners to his fold because there is none without sin except him and Jesus. Churches have no right to tell anyone whether they can worship or not. They do not have the right to judge a person or hold any wrongdoings against them. God forgives ALL! God loves All no matter their sins. HE is the ultimate Father and loves us unconditionally as we should love others. Everyone should be welcome in a church. This house of God is not ours its God's and the moment it becomes human property is the moment that the building becomes just another empty building.

So then you are no longer strangers and aliens, but you are fellow citizens with the saints and members of the household of God, built on the foundation of the apostles and prophets, Christ Jesus himself being the cornerstone, in whom the whole structure, being joined together, grows into a holy temple in the Lord. In Him you also are being built together into a dwelling place for God by the Spirit.

Ephesians 2:19-22

Chapter 7

Highway
of Prayer

Call to Me and I
will answer you, and will
tell you great and hidden
things that you have not
known.

Jeremiah 33:3

Prayer is an important part
in my life. I don't always remember what
or who to pray for but I believe God
knows. It calms me and fills me with His
presence. Prayer is just me talking to God,

no set rules. I pray to Him just walking around, sitting and crocheting, showering, or lying in bed at night awake. I talk to Him all the time. He always answers if I just listen to Him.

Early in our marriage we had Andy. He was born in Germany. As Andy got older he started asking for a sibling. I wanted another baby too. I prayed to God almost daily for another baby but it just wasn't happening.

One day I was feeling like I was in another world, a strange kind of focus on something beyond my sight. That day I decided that Andy was my world and if he is all God wanted me to have then so be it. I would be happy with that and thank the Lord for what I did have.

At some point that day while I was alone I went into my bedroom, knelt, and started praying. I told God that I except that if He wanted me to only have one child then I would let it go and be happy with my blessing of Andy. I told Him I did want more children and that it was becoming a burden that I was making myself carry by wanting another child so much. And for the first time I fully laid my burden onto the Lord to take care of. I released all that went with that burden onto Him and felt Him touch me, hug me and fill my heart.

Me being me however had put stipulations on it. Fortunately God knows me and still listens.

#1   I told him that if there was to be another child that I really didn't want to find out till I was far along, cause I knew the wait would kill me.

#2 I would like a girl, beautiful, healthy preferably with blue eyes.

#3 I would like her to resemble her daddy and Andy with dark hair.

#4 I wanted to find out on Lance's birthday to surprise him.

Silly you might think but it was my way of ending the burden. He already knew what was in my heart but for me I had to say it out loud. God always knows our prayer before we pray.

After I was done praying I realized I had somehow become prostrate on the floor, face down in the carpet, arms outstretched. So I just laid there and took it all in. I felt lighter, happier, and burden free. I verbally accepted the fate of the prayer either way. It was such a surreal moment and feeling to trust in God so completely and fully that I actually had handed Him my burden and all that came with it. No more worrying about Andy getting too old to have a sibling. Or me too old to be raising kids since by this time I was in my thirties.

And what do you think happened with that prayer? I can tell you that it was answered.

The next year when Andy was nine I started feeling very drained, sick and crampy all the time. I was scared something was wrong with me. See I was born with Polycystic Ovarian Syndrome or PCOS. And with this syndrome the doctors were finding that it affected one's heart, liver and kidneys and made us less likely to conceive, and you gain weight no matter what you try not to.

I had just started the first type of treatment (no cure) about seven months earlier. I dropped so much weight I went from 225 to 155 in a few months and didn't do anything special for it. But now I was worried about my internal organs. My period didn't come that month either, which not uncommon but on the medication all came on time, every time. Now because It was normal, before the medication to go months without a period I knew what to do. Normally my doctor who is the most wonderful doctor in the world would give me birth control and I would double up on pills for a few days and poof my period would start. All's well that ends well. I took pregnancy test before this, always just to make sure. It was a habit I still have. Even now in my forties I do it but maybe not as much now.

It was November 12th and Lance's birthday. See his birthday falls on hunting season and on the 12th every year he would go to hunting camp with his father and some family friends up in Missouri. His dad would buy his hunting license for his birthday present and this was a tradition that dates way back to his grandfather Mason. Lance would spend up to a week at deer camp depending on how long it took to fill his tag. Our anniversary also happen to fall on November 14th so usually I spent our anniversary alone. I think he planned that!

Anyways that year in 2003 Lance had to work (he was a OTR truck driver) He didn't come home until his dad had already left for deer camp. So since we only had one car I drove Lance up there when he got home that day and dropped him off.

I stopped at a liquor store and picked up a cold bottle of strawberry Champagne. I had never had champagne so I was going to have it tonight. I stopped at the video store and picked up a handful of my favorite movies. Then went to Walmart and got my favorite snacks, and a pregnancy test.

I got home, and put my stuff away and the champagne into the freezer to chill. It was getting late so I went into the bathroom peed on the stick and set it down and went about trying to open the bottle of champagne and get my snacks and movie ready. I went back to check the test and throw it away since it always was negative. But as you guessed it was different this time. There were two lines instead of one.

At first I thought they might have changed the tests and now two lines meant not pregnant. So I read the box and it said two lines pregnant one line not pregnant. Even though I had peed on the stick I still think I peed my pants a bit. I started to freak out and I paced the house over and over trying to wrap my mind around it. My test kit came with two test so I did it again and got the same results. So I figured out at this point that I was in fact pregnant.

To make a long story short It was Lance's birthday and I called him and surprised him with the news. He was as shocked as I was. We went to my doctor after he got home from his hunting trip and she confirmed I was indeed pregnant. She set me up with an OBGYN in Mountain Home. I had calculated by my last period that I should be somewhere around 6-8 weeks along.

The OBGYN gave me an ultrasound that day and discovered I was almost five and a half months along and it was a girl. And on May 3, 2004 Olivia Nicole came into this world and she had the bluest eyes and dark hair. She also looked like her daddy and Andy. Talk about in your face prayer answered. God listened to me and everything I asked for he gave me!

Don't ever underestimate the power of prayer. And don't overthink it, just do it, talk to him.

Several years later Andy (being an adult now) came to work with me here in Texas. After a few months he asked if he could bring a friend out to work with us. This friend had no real family, was homeless or stayed with friends off and on, no driver's license etc. I agreed but with the knowledge that if this kid needed to be fired Andy was doing it. With that John came into our lives.

After several more months God weighed it on my heart that John was alone in this world weather by his choice or by others. His dad passed away and his mom did also. He was mixed up. He had anxiety problems, but overall he was a great kid. But the fact that he had no family hurt me to the core of my mother's being.

And then God spoke to me. The idea of adopting John who by the way was 23, sounded like a great solution. Problem was I never thought Lance would go for it. But It was on my mind for months, I attempted to ask Lance about it but kept getting scared that he would say no. However God's will is always done in the end.

Me and Lance were driving to the RV store to get stuff for our fifth wheel since we were to leave for Arkansas soon for vacation. God at that very moment told me to ask him about John. I became anxious, my palms were sweating and I became withdrawn because I was scared to open my mouth. I wasn't scared of Lance in anyway, it was the idea that I felt this adoption needed to happen and he could say no and I would have to honor that. Lance had to be 100% on board with this.

After a few minutes I finally said to God in my head, Ok if you are really saying I need to do this and you really want this done then have Lance ask me what I am thinking about.

Not even a minute later Lance looked at me and said, "What are you thinking about"? In a flash my anxiety, sweats and fears left me. I was actually sitting there looking at him blankly in disbelief that God had just did this. I know that Lance's Angel had made him listen to God's will even if Lance didn't know it was God's will.

I started to laugh and told him, "you're not going to believe this but I have something to talk to you about. But I was scared you would say no. It has been on my heart for a while to talk to you about it." I explained that it had been on my heart but like Jonah, who tried to not do what God put on his heart, in the end His will is done!

I told Lance my wants of adopting John and to my surprise he more shocked about the God thing then the adoption. He promptly agreed that adoption was the right thing for us and John. So I went to the kids and asked them first if it was ok with them for John to become their real brother and all three jumped and said yes!

I approached John later that day, afraid he would say no. But I had more confidence that this is what God wanted so I just asked him. He excitedly said yes and on March 9th seven days

before my birthday John Mario became
our oldest son.

About a year and a half later
things were going really bad with the
company we worked for. We loved them
but it was getting to the point that we
were becoming more slaves then workers.
We would of done anything for this
company. But it seemed something
changed. Lance was working on a new
project for the company and the people he
was working with just really made him
fall in love with this company.
He had a hard time deciding
what the right thing was. He was
concerned for our boss' whom he loved
dearly and had worked for, for a long
time. After many weeks of prayers one
morning he got down on his knees and
prayed to God to lead him where he
needed to go. And to help him make the
right decision. Shortly thereafter the new
company came to him and offered him a
job. He took that as a sign and needless to
say we have been very happy since.
I believe that this was the
first time that Lance had totally entrusted
a decision to God and the results were just
as they had been for me in the past. That
total surrendering of one's self I think is
when God listens the most. Those prayers
are like rockets to heaven, protected and
shine the brightest.

Prayer is powerful,
when you pray your Angel will kneel

before you and pray with you. Prayers to me go to God in streaks of light up to heaven. I can imagine it looking like a highway of prayers. But Satan and his minions want to stop that prayer from getting to God. So the stronger your heart and connection with God the stronger your prayer is on its journey to heaven. And the more people that pray together the stronger the prayer becomes. Even Satan can't get it if it's powerful enough.

I love to pray all the time. It's more like talking with my best friend. I have an earthly father whom I love very much. But my Heavenly Father is forever and His love is greater for me than anyone could even come close to matching.

So pray and pray often, talk to your Father in heaven. Give Him your burdens and your fears. Tell Him what's going on in your life, even though He knows. He loves to hear us talk to Him. He loves to see the prayers come to Him. He may already know what's on your heart but He still likes to hear it from your heart.

The road as a Christian was never promised to be easy. We try to get through life one day at a time. There are many of us in this world who have bad times and some really bad times. There are people in the world that go through so much pain on a daily basis that most of us could not comprehend or understand. God puts us right where we need to be, when we need to be. It is up to us what we do with our lives and the time we have here.

I hope that when I stand before God and all of his glory I can at least say Yes Father I tried! We are not perfect and without sin. But we are perfectly made and loved without condition. No man can lead us to heaven except Christ our Lord. It is only by him and the grace of God that there is a place waiting for us that is perfect beyond our wildest imaginations. A place of peace and beauty.

This is just a small part of my story and how God got me to where I am today. My beliefs are reality to me not something I change as I need, but add to as I go through life and God reveals things to us. The bible is our guide, God is our father and leader who deserves our never ending loyalty.

We are a huge dysfunctional family, but family nonetheless. Sin is something we deal with and are tested on daily basis. It is who we are and what we are that matters. Even Angels and Archangels fall to sin. No one it without temptation to the evils of this world.

Evil is easy, Satan makes it that way so that it will be easy for us to turn to his lies and temptations with little effort. He is the great Deceiver in our world and him and his minions will be here on Earth until the next coming of the Lord. He himself is guilty of sin along with other Angels and Archangels.

But we are not without help in this battle for our souls. God gives us

the power over evil just by invoking Jesus'
name. He gives us his written word and an
angel to guide us.

Not all battles are on the
front lines. Most of the important battles
are within ourselves. So be true to God
and remember that he created every
living soul on this Earth. Respect that,
love that and honor that.

My advice is to live a good
life, praise God often, talk to him and let
him in. And remember that all beings are
of God's creation and all deserve to be
loved as you are loved by the creator
himself.

May God bless you and keep
you, may you always try to walk the path
of righteousness and uphold the love of
God! May you do for others no matter
what they have done for you. May God
protect you and fill you with his love and
glory!

Be very careful,
then, how you live—not as
unwise but as wise, making
the most of every
opportunity, because the
days are evil.
Therefore do not
be foolish, but understand
what the Lord's will is.
Do not get drunk
on wine, which leads to
debauchery. Instead, be
filled with the Spirit,
speaking to one
another with psalms,
hymns, and songs from the
Spirit. Sing and make music
from your heart to the Lord,
always giving
thanks to God the Father for
everything, in the name of
our Lord Jesus Christ.

Ephesians 5:15-20

This book is not
professionally edited or changed in any
way. You will find spelling errors,
grammar error and maybe a repeat or
two. But it's my story and it is how I wish
it to be published.

email:fortheloveofgodmyfaithfuljourny@
gmail.com
                    Or
Look us up on Facebook For the Love of
God: My faithful Journey